Hitting a

Living in a Violent Family

FRAN PICKERING

The
Children's
Society

First published in 2000

The Children's Society
Edward Rudolf House
Margery Street
London WC1X 0JL

Website: www.the-childrens-society.org.uk

Artwork by Annabel Tziros
Cover art by Katie Hall
Design and layouts by John Pickering
Typeset by Technical Art Services

The Children's Society is a registered charity:
Charity Registration No. 221124.

A catalogue record of this book is available
from the British Library.

ISBN 1 899783 21 0

Fran Pickering has asserted her right under
the Copyright, Designs and Patents Act 1988
to be identified as the author of this work.

Contents

ACKNOWLEDGEMENT

The Children's Soctiety would like to thank the
women and children of Lyncroft House Refuge, Birmingham,
for their help in producing this book.

Is this book for me?

If you live in a home where one of the adults often hits, kicks or punches the other adult...

If you live in a home where an adult often hits you . . .

If your older brother or sister hits you...

If you live in a home where you always have to watch what you say or do ...

If your mother often has cuts, bruises or broken limbs because your father or her boyfriend hits her...

If you and your mother have left home because your father or stepfather kept hitting her or you ...

If some of these things have happened to you ...

THEN THIS BOOK IS FOR YOU!

If you have a friend who worries about these things...

THEN THIS BOOK IS FOR THEM!

What's happening at home?

You are not alone

Getting hurt and being scared are terrible things to live with – and even worse if you can't tell anyone.

What can you do if these things are happening to you?

The first thing you need to know is that you are not alone.

There are many people, adults **and** children, who have gone through the same thing but it can be very difficult to talk about it.

There are many other people who know what it's like to feel afraid and unhappy.

You may have a friend who is worried about these things.

There is a way out. There is help.

Don't worry, Zippy, we care what happens to you. Read this book and find out you are not alone.

What is going on?

My dad comes home drunk and hits my mum. Sometimes she ends up in hospital.

My stepdad breaks my toys.

My dad takes drugs and then shouts at me and my brother. He tells us we're no good.

My mum's partner won't let her go out and meet her friends. He won't give her any money to spend.

My mum gets stressed and hits us.

My dad kicks my dog and that makes me cry.

My dad's always telling my mum she's a useless mother.

When adults hit or bully each other, it is called 'domestic violence'.

Is this right?

No! Bullying and cruelty are never right. No matter *who* is doing it. It can even be against the law.

Hitting someone is **wrong!**

Kicking and punching someone is **wrong!**

Making someone feel afraid all the time is **wrong!**

Touching someone where they don't want to be touched is **wrong!**

You have a right to be safe and feel safe – especially in your own home.

If someone is hurting *you*, call the NSPCC helpline.

See page 37

See page 25

How I feel

I'm scared

I'm afraid to go home because they are always fighting.

I don't feel safe at home.

I'm afraid of him.

I'm afraid of her.

I'm scared my sister will get hurt.

I try and hide from him.

I can't relax. I never know what he'll pick on next.

I feel like running away. I don't want to live with this fear inside.

I sit on the stairs and listen to them fighting.

What is happening to you at home is WRONG. That's why you feel scared all the time. Read this book and TELL SOMEONE what's going on.

It makes me angry

She's my mum but she can't stop him.

She doesn't listen to me. But when she's on her own she gives us attention.

See pages 20–21 >

Most of the time she just leaves us to it, but we're only kids.

I just want to kick his face in.

I hate him – I wish he'd die.

See pages 22–23 >

She's so wrapped up in her own stuff she can't see what it's doing to me. I take it out on my brother.

It makes me want to smash things up.

I wish someone would beat him up.

When the people who should be looking after you are *hurting* you, it makes you angry. You have a right to be angry.

My tummy hurts

I feel sick when I know he's coming home.

Sometimes I can't take in what people are saying to me.

My head aches and I can't think straight. I can't do my school work.

I can't sleep and I have bad dreams.

I'm not hungry.

I don't want to go out to play.

I shake a lot.

I feel tired all the time. I wake up crying.

My tummy hurts.

When you are sad, afraid or worried about what's going to happen next, your body feels bad too. TELL SOMEONE. If you can't explain very well, ask them to read this book.

I don't know what I feel

I feel like I'm going to burst with the stuff in my head.

I love him in a way because he's my dad.

Sometimes he's nice, but he gets mad – then I hate him.

I can't cry. I can't laugh. I don't feel anything.

I feel muddled – I don't know what I feel.

I don't feel anything. It feels like it's happening to someone else.

I say I'm OK but I'm not.

I love him but I want him to stop hitting mum.

Zippy feels confused.

It's all my fault

Everything I do is wrong. I get picked on all the time.

He doesn't like us playing or making a noise. He doesn't like us doing anything.

I keep out of the way – it's me he hates most.

My mum takes it out on me.

My mum says we can't leave because my wheelchair won't fit anywhere else.

It must be my fault.

I try to be good but nothing I do is right.

I deserve this. I'm to blame.

No, no, Zippy! It's not your fault. You have a right to be yourself, to play and have friends. No one should get angry with you just for that.

I feel responsible

I'm often left alone to look after my brothers and sisters.

I don't go to school. If anything happens to my mum she needs me there.

Sometimes I try to stop him but he only hits her more.

I don't want my brothers and sisters to see it.

If I do something wrong he hits her.

If I'm there perhaps I can stop him hitting her.

I look after the little ones because my mum can't cope.

You cannot take care of everything, Zippy. This is not your fault. You can get help. See page 37

What can I do about it?

What can I do? I'm only a kid.

I don't know what to do.

See page 18

Things you can do:

Draw pictures or write about how you feel.

Find a favourite toy and keep it with you.

TELL! TELL! TELL! It's OK to tell.

Talk to an adult you know and like.

Say to an adult: 'I want to talk to you.' Before you lose your nerve, say: 'My dad hits my mum and I don't like it.'

Talk to a friend. It helps to share your fears and worries.

See page 37 for the Childline number

It's affecting my life

This is really embarrassing

I sometimes wet my bed at night.

I'm afraid my mum will run away so I hang on to her all the time.

I cry a lot.

If I eat, I throw up.

I suck my thumb at school. The kids tease me but I can't stop it.

I hate my friends seeing my mum's bruises.

I wake up screaming in the night.

I just want my family to be normal.

It is NORMAL to do things like this when you are frightened and worried. You can't help it. None of this is your fault.

It's hard at school

I can't concentrate. I keep thinking about home.

I try to be good at school so they don't notice me.

The teachers are always getting at me about homework. I'm so tired I can't think.

The kids at school pick on me.

I can't go to school, people will see the bruises on my arms. I just bunk off.

The teachers have no idea, they just think I'm quiet.

Maybe they just think I'm thick.

My teacher just thinks I'm a bully.

TELL a teacher what is happening. They need to know. Then they can try and help you cope with school.

I can't tell anyone

No one would believe me.

I can't tell anyone because I'm ashamed.

I'll be taken away if I tell.

I can't get my dad into trouble.

I can't tell. I already get called names because I'm black – telling would make it even worse.

I don't want people to feel sorry for me.

My mum doesn't want the neighbours to know.

My dad'll kill me if I tell. He says it's our secret.

Zippy needs courage to tell.

Be brave, Zippy. It is NOT WRONG to tell someone. Tell someone you trust who will listen: a teacher, your aunt, a friend's parent, a grandparent. You need help. See page 37

How can I help my mum?

Show her this book. Give her lots of hugs.

She doesn't have to stay. You both need to escape from the fear and have time to think what to do next. There are safe places to go.  *Show her pages 26–27*

Not everyone has to leave. Mum can get the police to keep him away.

Tell her how it makes you feel. If she doesn't understand, show her the chapter called 'How I feel'.

Show her pages 7–12

Ask your mum to talk to someone who can help her get her head straight about it.

Show her page 37

If someone is hurting you or your mum, this should *not* be kept secret. Unless someone tells, this will go on. She can get help.

Trying to understand

Why does mum keep quiet about it?

Why does mum put up with it?

Why does mum let him hurt us?

Why does mum stay?

Why does mum put us through this?

Maybe she's ashamed. She doesn't want anyone to know what is going on.

Maybe she thinks he'll change. Maybe that's why she keeps forgiving him.

Maybe she thinks it's her fault. Maybe she believes him when he says he's sorry.

Maybe mum doesn't know how she will earn enough money to feed us all. She hasn't got anywhere for us to go.

Show her pages 26–27 and 37

Maybe it's because she doesn't speak very good English and that makes it harder to leave.

Maybe mum's so afraid she can't think straight.

Maybe she's afraid to leave in case he comes after her and hurts her more. Are there places to go where we will all be safe?

Tell your mum she is not alone. Other people have found a way out. She can too.

Why does he do it?

You don't expect your dad to hit your mum, do you?

You don't expect your dad to hurt you, do you?

Why should you be scared of your mum's boyfriend?

Sometimes people are violent because:

- They don't know how to deal with their own feelings, like anger or fear, so they hit someone to let the feelings out.

- Seeing someone afraid of them makes them feel big.

- They are bullies. They want to control another person.

- They grew up with a violent adult and think this is the way to treat people.

- They think it's OK to do this.

- They blame other people for what they are feeling inside.

- They feel jealous.

- They can't talk about how they feel.

**But hitting and hurting
another person is NEVER right.**

Beating, hurting and scaring another person are not ways an adult should behave. People who do this need to be stopped.

See page 25

Changes at home

He's got to stay away

Mum went for help.

See page 37

If someone is doing something that is against the law, they can be stopped.

A judge told dad he had to leave us alone. He has to live somewhere else.

If dad comes back and tries to hurt us, mum can call the police – they will help mum keep dad away.

We may be able to see dad, but only in a safe place.

Zippy has a right to be safe in his home.

We've left home

We left home in a hurry.

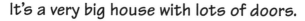

We're in a refuge.

It's a very big house with lots of doors.

When we got here a lady met us and gave us a room to stay in.

Now we've got a big room with our beds in.

We share a bathroom with other families.

We have our own bathroom and kitchen.

My mum cooks our meals in a big kitchen that the other mums use.

There are people to talk to here.

We eat in our room.

We eat in a dining room with other mums and kids.

There are other kids here to be friends with. We can play and make a noise here.

We can't have anyone to visit us here because the address is a secret.

We feel safe and can sleep well.

Now you have come to stay at a refuge things can get better. Here you can sleep and play and be safe.

Everything's strange and I can't cope

I don't like it here. Everything's strange.

I don't know what's happening or what to expect.

I don't know how to behave here.

I have to go to a new school. I won't know anyone.

No one tells me what's going on.

How long will we be here?

See page 30

There are too many people here.

I get confused. Everything is different now.

Leaving home in a hurry and facing all the new things is very scary. There's a lot to cope with, but each day it will get a little easier.

I feel so sad

I miss my dad. I know he hit her but I miss him.

I miss my dog. I couldn't bring him with me.

I don't talk much here. I'm scared of crying in front of them.

I miss my friends. I didn't get a chance to say goodbye.

Even my nan doesn't know where we are in case dad finds out.

I had to leave my toys and my computer behind.

I feel so sad, it hurts.

I feel empty inside.

Losing things we love makes us very, very sad. Tell someone how sad you feel. Draw a picture of what you miss.

What next?

You won't need to be scared any more. You can play and have fun.

You can sleep and feel safe.

Your mum will start to feel better and be happier again.

Soon your mum will find a new home for you to live in.

You'll make new friends and have them home to play.

Your mum has made changes to your life so you can be safe. She has a chance to make things better.

Life can get better now, Zippy.

The future

Will I ever be happy?

Yes – hurting and sadness isn't all there is, even if it is all you've known.

When you have a bad cut it hurts, but it soon heals. Inside you is like that.

Talking to someone will help you cope.

Soon this will all be over and you'll be having fun with your friends.

You can go out and have fun with your nan or your aunt or uncle.

You and your mum will start to do new things in your new home.

There are still lots of things to enjoy. You will soon forget the bad times.

I don't want the same thing to happen to me

It doesn't have to. You can choose.

You can choose to look at this page or you can choose to put the book down – **you** can decide.

If someone says you're stupid or ugly, you can choose to listen – or you can walk away.

If your friend tries to bully you by making you do what they want, you can refuse and find a better friend.

Always, even if it seems hard, you can choose what to do.

Your thoughts are yours. You can choose.

I don't want to be like my dad

It's your choice how you behave. No one *makes* people hit each other. They choose to do it.

Just because your dad is violent, it doesn't mean you will be too.

Feelings are like the fizz in a bottle of pop. If you shake the bottle too much, all the fizz bursts out.

It is hard to learn how to deal with feelings, but here are some ways to let the fizz out a bit at a time.

• Talking to someone helps you work out how you really feel – it often helps you find a way to make things better.

- Try talking about how you feel to a friend or adult you know well.

- Talk to a pet. Never, ever, hit a pet because you feel angry – it's not their fault.

- Punch a pillow.

- Go outside somewhere safe and run around.

- Scribble hard on a piece of paper, screw the paper up and throw it as far as you can.

Anger, fear and jealousy are strong feelings. They can fizz up and come out in the wrong way.

It's OK and normal to feel these things. But it's NOT OK to hit someone because of how you feel.

Remember, you can choose. You can decide *how* to let the fizz out. NEVER let it out on someone else.

Where to get help

Remember, you are not alone. There are people who can help and who will listen to you.

You can ring one of these free phone numbers:

- **Childline: 0800 1111**
- **NSPCC helpline: 0800 800 500**
- **If there is fighting and you are scared, ring 999.**

You can tell an adult you know and trust:

- a teacher
- a grandparent
- an aunt or uncle
- a friend of mum or dad
- a friend's parent
- a friend – and ask them to tell their mum or dad
- a leader at the youth club
- the local vicar
- a police officer
- a social worker
- the school nurse
- a health visitor.

Mum can get help from:

- Women's Aid helpline: **0345 023 468**
- Refuge 24-hour National Helpline: **0870 599 5443**
- the Citizen's Advice Bureau
- a solicitor
- the police
- the local social services and housing departments
- local domestic violence advice centres.

Notes for adults

INTRODUCTION

Violence in the home affects everyone who lives there – children as well as adults. Violence in the home occurs in all social classes and in all ethnic groups, and the problem is widespread.

Children may experience harm directly or indirectly. In around seven out of ten homes where there is domestic violence, children are also being abused. Where there is domestic violence, there are often other types of abuse happening as well.

Violence in the home is still shrouded in secrecy, shame and embarrassment: there is a taboo about talking about it. But avoiding or ignoring the problem allows it to continue to damage children and continue the cycle.

Hitting and Hurting: Living in a Violent Family has been developed by staff and young people from The Children's Society's Wyrley Birch Project, Birmingham, in response to the needs of children who have lived with, or are living with, violence.

Children who are keeping the secret of violence may find a way to tell someone through reading this book; it acknowledges their feelings, makes it clear that it is not their fault, and suggests ways of dealing with the difficult feelings they have been left with.

Parents, relatives, family friends, teachers, school nurses, social workers and other child welfare staff who live with, or work with, children will also find this book a useful resource.

Guidance notes

A word of caution – please note that this book is not 'diagnostic' – that is, a child who displays some of the behaviours and emotions noted in this book may be doing so for reasons other than domestic violence.

For adults using this book with children, there are no hard and fast ways of using it, but please note the following points:

* the book can be read in stages on different occasions;

* don't make a child read this book if they don't want to;

* don't make a child talk if they don't want to, but encourage them to talk at a later date if they want to;

* reassure a child that they can ask any questions they want;

* let them read the book on their own if they would prefer this;

* be ready if a child tells you about violence they are living with;

* if a child asks a question you don't know the answer to then be honest, but agree that you will find out the answer for them;

* don't panic or over-react – if you do it will make the child feel worse and less confident about your ability to help;

* ALWAYS take the child's concerns seriously and agree with them that you will make sure the best people to help are told.

If a child tells you about abuse they are experiencing – or you have good reason to think they are experiencing abuse of any kind – this information must be shared with the agencies that can investigate your concerns: your local social services department or the police.

This means you cannot promise a child complete confidentiality before they talk to you. However, children deserve respect and to have their views taken into account: they should be consulted and kept informed throughout the information-sharing and decision-making processes.

The book is designed to be read by children without adult help, but it can also be used by adults working with younger children by using the illustrations to construct a story to help the child explore their own experience of living in a violent home.

This book covers a range of situations and emotions that children commonly experience when they live with domestic violence. But not every child will have the same experiences or react in the same way: each child will also have different ways of trying to make sense of their experiences. For children who are not living with violence, this book can help them understand what it's like for children who are.

Sheena Doyle
Programme Manager, The Children's Society

A positive force for change

The Children's Society is one of Britain's leading charities for children and young people. Founded in 1881 as a Christian organisation, The Children's Society reaches out unconditionally to children and young people regardless of race, culture or creed.

Over 100 projects throughout England and Wales

We work with over 40,000 children of all ages, focusing on those whose circumstances have made them particularly vulnerable. We aim to help to stop the spiral into isolation, anger and lost hope faced by so many young people.

We constantly look for effective, new ways of making a real difference

We measure local impact and demonstrate through successful practice that major issues can be tackled and better resolved. The Children's Society has an established track record of taking effective action: both in changing public perceptions about difficult issues such as child prostitution, and in influencing national policy and practice to give young people a better chance at life.

The Children's Society is committed to overcoming injustice wherever we find it

We are currently working towards national solutions to social isolation, lack of education and the long-term problems they cause, through focused work in several areas:

* helping parents whose babies and toddlers have inexplicably stopped eating, endangering their development;

* involving children in the regeneration of poorer communities;

* preventing exclusions from primary and secondary schools;

* providing a safety net for young people who run away from home and care;

* seeking viable alternatives to the damaging effects of prison for young offenders.

The Children's Society will continue to raise public awareness of difficult issues to promote a fairer society for the most vulnerable children in England and Wales. For further information about the work of The Children's Society or to obtain a publications catalogue, please contact:

The Children's Society, Publishing Department, Edward Rudolf House, Margery Street, London WC1X 0JL. Tel. 0207 841 4400. Fax 0207 841 4500.

Website: www.the-childrens-society.org.uk

The Children's Society is a registered charity: Charity Registration No. 221124.